MAMA NEEDS A MARTINI!

MAMA NEEDS A MARTINI!

Cocktail Recipes for When Motherhood Is Tough as a Mother

BAILEY KOESTER

Photography by
RICK LUETTKE

Skyhorse Publishing

To the loves of my life (and reasons I drink), Smitty and Glen.

CONTENTS

INTRODUCTION

Mama needs a martini: My catchphrase turned cocktail book. Between being a first-time mom trying to figure out what the heck I'm doing and attempting to form a bond with our newest, noisiest, yet most adorable roommate, my catchphrase became one of celebration and one of defeat. Baby slept through the night? Mama needs a martini! Baby had an up-the-back and down-the-legs blowout? Mama needs a martini! It was a phrase that worked for every occasion and, to be honest, a martini just felt right. Like a rite of passage into this wild ride called motherhood.

There will be days (and weeks) when you feel like the motherhood gods are against you and smiting you for every terrible thing you ever did to your parents. Always remember, everything is temporary, and most phases go just as quickly as they came. May your glass never be empty and may there always be more martinis of celebration than martinis of defeat. Cheers, Mama!

CHAPTER 1
Salty, Sour & Citrus Cocktails

NEW YORK, NEW YORK

Technically a New York Sour (but the name New York, New York is so much catchier, don't you think?) Not only is this cocktail delicious and beautiful, it is also the perfect prop for a selfie when your hair and makeup are so on point (a rarity these days) that you have to document it. You do you, girl!

MAKES 1 SERVING

Ingredients

2 ounces whisky
1 ounce lemon juice
½ ounce simple syrup
Ice
Splash dry red wine

Instructions

1. Combine the whisky, lemon juice, and simple syrup in an ice-filled cocktail shaker.

2. Shake until chilled.

3. Strain into an ice-filled rocks glass.

4. Slowly pour red wine on top to float.

5. Gently stir if desired.

PUCKER UP

I don't always have grapefruit juice in my fridge, but, when I do, this is my go-to cocktail. It's a must-try! Actually, do yourself a favor and pick your favorite version from the Pro Mom Tip below.

MAKES 1 SERVING

Ingredients

1 ounce grapefruit juice
½ ounce lime juice
¾ ounce simple syrup
Drizzle honey
Pinch salt
1½ ounces vodka
Ice

Instructions

1. Combine the grapefruit juice, lime juice, simple syrup, honey, salt, and vodka in an ice-filled cocktail shaker and shake until chilled.

2. Strain into a chilled coupe glass.

PRO MOM TIP

Swap out the vodka for tequila and have yourself a honey paloma! Out of both? Try a light rum. Prefer gin? Try it and make your own version of a Greyhound cocktail. So versatile!

THE REAL DAIQUIRI

I can't possibly be the only person who thought a proper daiquiri came out of one of those frozen slushie machines, right? Apparently real daiquiris, like this one, have been around for more than one hundred years! Mix one of these up and sit back and enjoy.

MAKES 1 SERVING

Ingredients

2 ounces white rum
1 ounce lime juice
½ ounce simple syrup
Ice

Instructions

1. Combine the white rum, lime juice, and simple syrup in an ice-filled cocktail shaker and shake until chilled.

2. Strain into a chilled coupe or martini glass.

PRO MOM TIP

Feeling crazy? Add a splash of grapefruit juice.

BALSAMIC BERRY

Fun fact: The process of combining fresh fruit with vinegar to use as the basis of a beverage dates all the way back to colonial times. Now that we have our history lesson out of the way, it's time for a cocktail. Basil and strawberries were meant for each other (and this cocktail), but the sweet and tangy balsamic vinegar is the real star of this show.

MAKES 1 SERVING

Ingredients

3 strawberries

5 basil leaves

1½ ounces gin or vodka

Small splash balsamic vinegar

1 pinch black pepper

Ice

Splash dry sparkling wine

Instructions

1. Muddle the strawberries and basil in a cocktail shaker.

2. Add the gin or vodka, balsamic vinegar, black pepper, and ice.

3. Shake until chilled.

4. Strain into an ice-filled tall glass and top with sparkling wine.

FRENCH 75

The French 75 cocktail is named after a field gun used during World War I that revolutionized modern artillery. The only way to make this badass cocktail even more badass is to slice open your bottle of bubbly with a saber. (I'm not recommending that but, if you do, I want to watch.)

MAKES 2 SERVINGS

Ingredients

2 ounces gin
½ ounce simple syrup
½ ounce lemon juice
Ice
Splash sparkling wine

Instructions

1. Combine gin, simple syrup, and lemon juice in an ice-filled cocktail shaker.

2. Shake until chilled.

3. Strain into two champagne flutes and top with sparkling wine.

SALTED ALMOND

Despite there only being half an ounce of amaretto in this recipe, it tastes just like a salted almond. Don't ask me how the rest of the ingredients work together to achieve this flavor, because I honestly have no idea. What I do know, though, is that it's a great alternative to an overly sweet after-dinner drink.

MAKES 1 SERVING

Ingredients

1½ ounce tequila

½ ounce amaretto

1 ounce grapefruit juice

½ ounce lime juice

2 dashes orange bitters

1 *teeny-tiny* pinch salt

Ice

Instructions

1. Combine the tequila, amaretto, grapefruit juice, lime juice, bitters, and salt in an ice-filled cocktail shaker.

2. Shake well for 30 seconds.

3. Strain into a chilled coupe glass.

TEAQUILA

No, not a typo. There's tea in this cocktail! Inspired by my daily tumbler full of iced tea (and love of tequila?), the Teaquila was born. Though similar to a hot toddy, this recipe won't magically cure your cold and soothe your sore throat—sorry—but I can promise that you'll be feeling really good after a couple of these!

MAKES 1 SERVING

Ingredients

2 ounces unsweetened black tea

1½ ounces tequila

½ ounce simple syrup

½ ounce lemon juice

2 dashes aromatic bitters (optional)

Ice

Instructions

1. Combine the black tea, tequila, simple syrup, lemon juice, and aromatic bitters (if using) in an ice-filled cocktail shaker.

2. Shake and strain into an ice-filled glass.

BISHOP

Originally created by Charles H. Baker, Jr., known for being a hustler who was better at drinking cocktails than making them, the Bishop is another oldie but easy-to-make cocktail with easily accessible ingredients. Cheers to Charlie, the guy who I can only imagine would have been my best friend if I was alive one hundred years ago.

MAKES 1 SERVING

Ingredients

3 ounces dark rum
1 ounce bold, dry red wine
1 teaspoon simple syrup
½ ounce lime juice
Ice

Instructions

1. Combine the rum, wine, simple syrup, and lime juice in an ice-filled cocktail shaker.

2. Shake until chilled.

3. Strain into a wineglass or rocks glass over ice.

THE CLASSIC

This is my go-to cocktail. The one thing that never lets me down. I look forward to it after a long, hard day. Hell, I look forward to it after an easy day, too. The key is making it *lightly* dirty, like thigh-high-patent-leather-boots-and-a-mini-skirt-but-still-goes-to-church-on-Sundays dirty.

MAKES 1 SERVING

Ingredients

4 ounces vodka

Splash olive juice

Ice

Blue cheese–stuffed olives, to garnish

Instructions

1. Combine the vodka and olive juice in an ice-filled cocktail shaker.

2. Shake for 20 to 30 seconds.

3. Strain into a chilled martini glass.

4. Garnish with blue cheese–stuffed olives.

PRO MOM TIP

This cocktail is not complete without blue cheese–stuffed olives. This is for two reasons: one, cocktails are obviously always better with food, and two, this is one food your adorable little crumb snatcher will not steal from you (or will likely quickly regret stealing from you).

 B & B

This recipe is easy to make and husband-approved (if you feel like sharing). Inspired by the classic boilermaker cocktail, we add a bit of sweet (simple syrup) and sour (lemon juice) and combine it all into one glass to round this drink out.

MAKES 1 SERVING

Ingredients

2 ounces bourbon
Splash lemon juice
½ teaspoon simple syrup
Dash aromatic bitters
Ice
1 (12-ounce) bottle lager beer

Instructions

1. Combine the bourbon, lemon juice, simple syrup, and bitters in an ice-filled cocktail shaker and shake until chilled.

2. Strain into a chilled glass.

3. Fill glass with beer.

BABY PINK

If there's ever a time in your life when you want to impress someone by combining a bunch of random sh*t together to make a fancy cocktail, here's your recipe. Bonus points for using the vintage glasses you found in your grandma's basement.

MAKES 1 SERVING

Ingredients

¾ ounce gin

1 teaspoon triple sec

1 teaspoon simple syrup

1 tablespoon lemon juice

2 teaspoons apple juice

Ice

Splash sparkling rosé wine

Instructions

1. Combine the gin, triple sec, simple syrup, and juices in an ice-filled cocktail shaker.

2. Shake until chilled.

3. Strain into a fancy vintage glass or champagne flute.

4. Top with sparkling wine.

JOSÉ AND ROSÉ

An orange margarita with a splash of rosé to cool off? Yes, please! Cue Julie Andrews, because "these are a few of my favorite things. . . ."

MAKES 1 SERVING

Ingredients

1½ ounces tequila
½ ounce triple sec
½ ounce blood orange juice
½ ounce lime juice
Ice
Splash rosé wine

Instructions

1. Combine the tequila, triple sec, and juices in an ice-filled cocktail shaker.

2. Shake until chilled and strain into a chilled tall glass.

3. Top with wine.

PARDON ME . . .

Yes, I was eating sandwiches while experimenting with various cocktail recipes for this book. Yes, this is the result of those experimentations. Yes, I had already been drinking. If you don't judge me and this cocktail, I won't judge you.

MAKES 1 SERVING

Ingredients

2 ounces white rum
¾ ounce lemon juice
½ teaspoon Dijon mustard
1 ounce honey
Ice

Instructions

1. Combine the rum, lemon juice, mustard, and honey in an ice-filled cocktail shaker.

2. Shake until chilled.

3. Strain into a chilled coupe or martini glass.

TEQUILA SOUR

This Tequila Sour is the cocktail love child of a margarita and a lemon meringue pie. Don't let the egg whites scare you off! They add a fluffy, foamy, meringue-like texture that I'm quite sure you'll love. If you're vegan or I just can't talk you into using egg whites, replace them with 2 tablespoons of aquafaba (the liquid from a can of chickpeas).

MAKES 1 SERVING

Ingredients

2 ounces gold tequila

1 ounce lemon juice

½ ounce simple syrup

1 dash aromatic bitters

1 egg white

Ice

Instructions

1. Combine the tequila, lemon juice, simple syrup, bitters, and egg white in a cocktail shaker without ice and shake vigorously for 30 seconds.

2. Add ice and shake again to chill.

3. Strain into a chilled coupe glass up or on the rocks.

LIQUID GOLD

I took the Amaretto Sour and gave it a more mature look with some dark rum and aromatic bitters.

MAKES 1 SERVING

Ingredients

1½ ounce whisky

¾ ounce dark rum

½ ounce lime juice

1 teaspoon simple syrup

1 teaspoon amaretto

1 dash aromatic bitters

Ice

Instructions

1. Combine the whisky, dark rum, lime juice, simple syrup, amaretto, and bitters in an ice-filled cocktail shaker.

2. Shake until chilled.

3. Strain into an ice-filled rocks glass.

CHAPTER 2
Savory & Spicy Cocktails

RED RUM

Go ahead and consider your daily fruit and vegetable intake complete after this cocktail. (You're welcome!) It's perfect for when you need to use up any leftover pepper or basil in your fridge. A win-win!

MAKES 1 SERVING

Ingredients

3 ounces grapefruit juice, *divided*
Coarse salt, to rim the glass
¼ red bell pepper, thinly sliced
8 basil leaves
Ice
2 ounces light rum
Splash club soda

Instructions

1. Wet the rim of a collins glass with grapefruit juice.

2. Pour a small pool of salt onto a plate or shallow dish and roll the rim of the glass in the salt to coat.

3. Fill the prepared glass with ice and set aside to chill in the refrigerator or freezer.

4. Muddle the bell pepper and basil in a cocktail shaker.

5. Fill the shaker with ice and add the rum and remaining grapefruit juice.

6. Shake vigorously until chilled and strain into your ice-filled collins glass.

7. Top with club soda.

CHILE WILLY

Even if you're not a fan of spicy heat in your drink, don't flip the page just yet. The lemon and bourbon are the star of this show, not the Ancho chile powder. You can even easily omit the chile-sugar rim, if you must, but you just might find yourself thoroughly enjoying it! This isn't a girly froufrou drink but it's classy AF and one that your significant other might even enjoy, too . . . if you feel like sharing.

MAKES 2 SERVINGS

Ingredients

1 ounce lemon juice, *divided*
1 teaspoon granulated sugar
¼ teaspoon ancho chile powder, *divided*
4 ounces bourbon
½ ounce triple sec
½ ounce simple syrup
Ice

Instructions

1. Wet the rim of two coupe glasses with lemon juice.

2. On a plate or shallow dish, mix together the sugar and chile powder and roll the rim of each glass into the chile-sugar mixture to coat.

3. Set prepared glasses aside to chill in the refrigerator or freezer.

4. Combine the bourbon, remaining lemon juice, triple sec, simple syrup, and remaining chile powder in an ice-filled cocktail shaker and shake until chilled.

5. Strain into the prepared glasses.

THE "MASTER CLEANSE"

The fad diet of this same name, initially developed in the 1940s, consisted in part of no food and a laxative tea. Was it healthy? Hardly. Will it help you lose weight? After spending a couple of agonizing hours in the bathroom, I'm sure. The 1940s can keep their diet. We'll keep this cocktail.

MAKES 1 SERVING

Ingredients

1 tablespoon sugar

1 teaspoon cayenne pepper

¾ ounce lemon juice, *divided*

Ice

3 ounces bourbon

1 ounce maple syrup

Instructions

1. Combine the sugar with the cayenne pepper and pour onto a plate or shallow dish.

2. Wet the rim of a rocks glass with lemon juice and roll the rim of the glass through the sugar and cayenne mixture.

3. Fill the prepared glass with ice and set aside.

4. Combine the bourbon, remaining lemon juice, and maple syrup in an ice-filled cocktail shaker.

5. Shake thoroughly until chilled and strain into the prepared glass.

REVOLVER

Despite the Revolver consisting of mostly hard liquor and having a badass name, I promise it will not put hair on your chest.

MAKES 1 SERVING

Ingredients

2 ounces whisky
½ ounce coffee liqueur
2 dashes orange bitters
Ice

Instructions

1. Combine the whisky, coffee liqueur, and bitters in an ice-filled cocktail shaker.

2. Shake well for 30 seconds.

3. Strain into an ice-filled rocks glass.

SPICY SHANDY

Whether it's dining out or whipping up tacos and nachos at home, Mexican food is always a crowd-pleaser. It's also entirely possible that I enjoy Mexican and Mexican-inspired cocktails just as much as (more than?) anything dipped in queso blanco. This beer cocktail is a quick and easy alternative to a margarita, one step fancier than a plain ol' beer, and the perfect pairing for chips and salsa.

MAKES 1 SERVING

Ingredients

½ ounce simple syrup

1 ounce tequila

½ ounce lemon juice

2 ounces pineapple juice

¼–½ teaspoon juice from jalapeño jar
(depending on how spicy you like it)

8 ounces pale ale

Ice, *optional*

Instructions

1. In a pint glass, combine the simple syrup, tequila, fruit juices, and jalapeño juice.

2. Stir well.

3. Fill the pint glass with ice (if using) and/or pale ale.

NOT A LATTE

I've always thought that having a coffee after dinner was the kind of thing only sophisticated old people did. (You know, the same kind of people that order the cheese plate for dessert.) The only way I can drink coffee after dinner and not be awake for the next twelve hours is if it's mixed with booze, so this is one of my takes on an after-dinner coffee.

MAKES 1 SERVING

Ingredients

1½ ounces cold brew

2 ounces dark rum

½ ounce coffee liqueur

½ ounce simple syrup

½ ounce lemon juice

Ice

1 egg white

Instructions

1. Combine the cold brew, dark rum, coffee liqueur, simple syrup, and lemon juice in an ice-filled cocktail shaker and shake until chilled.

2. Strain into an Irish coffee mug and empty out shaker.

3. Place the egg white into the empty cocktail shaker and shake the sh*t out of it for at least 30 seconds or until frothy.

4. Gently pour the egg white on top of the cocktail.

THYME FOR A COCKTAIL!

I love a corny pun almost as much as I love thyme, so it's only fitting that I took the "thyme" to tweak the French 75 (page 11) and come up with this limey, fizzy, floral beaut of a drink.

MAKES 2 SERVINGS

Ingredients

1½ tablespoons lime juice
4 sprigs fresh thyme
1 ounce simple syrup
4 ounces tequila
Splash dry sparkling wine

Instructions

1. Combine the lime juice and thyme in a cocktail shaker and muddle together.

2. Add the simple syrup, tequila, and ice.

3. Shake until chilled.

4. Double strain and pour equally into two chilled coupe glasses.

5. Top each glass with sparkling wine.

CUKE WITH A KICK

Refreshing but with a bit of an unexpected kick, I imagine this cocktail being served at a swanky spa while your toenails are being painted the perfect shade of pink and chilled cucumber slices are resting on your eyelids. But . . . I'm guessing that scenario is highly unlikely, and you look more like I do—hair in a messy bun, leaning over the kitchen counter, flipping through this very book. If you have warm weather, the need for a little zen, and a few minutes to prep, this is the cocktail for you.

MAKES 1 SERVING

Ingredients

2 slices cucumber

8–10 cilantro leaves

1 thin, deseeded slice fresh jalapeño

½ ounce lime juice

½ ounce simple syrup

2 ounces gin

Ice

Instructions

1. Place the cucumber, cilantro, and jalapeño into a cocktail shaker and muddle.

2. Add the lime juice, simple syrup, gin, and ice.

3. Shake until chilled.

4. Strain into a coupe or martini glass.

BLOODY HELL

Not to be confused with the movie of the same title (LOL—like you have time for movies anymore), the only way this cocktail will transport you to somewhere worse than hell is if your kid gets ahold of the blood orange and stains everything you love. If you haven't gotten on board the blood orange train yet, do it now. This cocktail is equally as delicious without the jalapeño, but that's the "hell" part of the name, so leave it in for the full experience!

MAKES 1 SERVING

Ingredients

1 large blood orange, juiced

1½ ounces bourbon

1 small, deseeded slice fresh jalapeño

½ ounce simple syrup

Ice

Splash citrus beer

Instructions

1. Combine the juice, bourbon, jalapeño slice, and simple syrup in an ice-filled cocktail shaker and shake until chilled.

2. Strain into a tall glass and top with the beer.

BEERGARITA

Cold and refreshing with a little zing, this drink will make your summertime cocktail dreams come true.

MAKES 1 SERVING

Ingredients

1 ounce lime juice, *divided*

Chile-lime seasoning, to rim the glass

Ice

Pinch salt

1 ounce tequila

12 ounces Mexican lager

Lime wedge, to garnish

PRO MOM TIP

Need some spice in your life? Add a dash or two of hot sauce!

Instructions

1. Wet the rim of a pint glass or other tall glass with lime juice.

2. Pour a small pool of chile-lime seasoning onto a plate or shallow dish and roll the rim of the glass into the seasoning to coat.

3. Fill the prepared glass with ice and set aside.

4. Add the lime juice and a pinch of salt to the prepared glass.

5. Pour in the tequila.

6. Top with the beer and garnish with a lime wedge.

WASABATINI

This is what happens when you're experimenting with cocktail recipes for your book and order takeout sushi. Hear me out, though. If it's acceptable to put hot sauce and jalapeños in cocktails, why not wasabi? It's just a teeny-tiny pinch and it fully disintegrates into the vodka. Okay, now that I've hopefully talked you into it, give it a shot! Make sure to serve with a spicy tuna roll.

MAKES 1 SERVING

Ingredients

1 small pinch wasabi paste

3 ounces vodka

1 ounce lemon juice

Splash simple syrup

Ice

Instructions

1. Place the wasabi paste and vodka in a cocktail shaker and shake until the wasabi is completely dissolved.

2. Add the lemon juice, simple syrup, and ice.

3. Shake until chilled and strain into a chilled martini glass.

SEÑOR PICKLE

If Bloody Marys are for brunch, then the Señor Pickle is for lunch. The spiciness from the hot sauce, the sourness from the pickle, and the kick from the tequila is exactly what you need to get you through a Sunday-afternoon cleaning frenzy before the in-laws come over.

MAKES 1 SERVING

Ingredients

½ ounce lime juice, *divided*
Coarse salt, to rim the glass
1½ ounces tequila
½ ounce simple syrup
Splash pickle juice
1 (or 2) dash(es) hot sauce
Ice
Pickle spear, to garnish

Instructions

1. Wet the rim of a rocks glass with lime juice.

2. Pour a small pool of salt onto a plate or shallow dish and roll the rim of the glass in the salt to coat.

3. In a cocktail shaker, combine the tequila, remaining lime juice, simple syrup, pickle juice, and hot sauce.

4. Add ice, shake well, and pour into a rocks glass.

5. Garnish with a pickle spear.

PRO MOM TIP

Let the pickle spear soak in tequila for a minute before garnishing your glass with it!

THE "W" SAUCE ONE

"W" sauce . . . because no one actually knows how to pronounce Worcestershire. Other than a Bloody Mary and this cocktail, the only time I've ever used W sauce was in this delicious Chex™ Party Mix (page 59). In my opinion, we really need to show W sauce some more regularly scheduled love. It works similarly to vinegar in this recipe and, because of our history lesson with the Balsamic Berry (page 8), we now know how perfect it is for a cocktail!

MAKES 1 SERVING

Ingredients

5 basil leaves

2 ounces white rum

½ ounce lime juice

½ ounce simple syrup

4 drops Worcestershire sauce

Ice

Splash sparkling wine

Instructions

1. Tear the basil into big pieces and place into a cocktail shaker.

2. Add the rum, lime juice, simple syrup, Worcestershire sauce, and ice to the same shaker.

3. Vigorously shake until chilled.

4. Strain into a chilled hurricane glass.

5. Top with sparkling wine.

CHEX™ PARTY MIX

Do yourself a favor and make this Chex™ Party Mix while you have the W sauce out!

Ingredients

1 stick unsalted butter

2 tablespoons Worcestershire sauce

2 teaspoons seasoning salt

1 teaspoon garlic powder

1 teaspoon onion powder

1 teaspoon paprika

6 cups rice or corn Chex™ cereal

3 cups wheat Chex™ cereal

2 cups rye chips

2 cups Cheez-It® crackers (I like the spicy variety!)

2 cups mini pretzel sticks

1 cup cashews or peanuts, roasted and salted

Instructions

1. Preheat the oven to 250°F.

2. In a microwave-safe bowl, warm the butter on low for about 15 to 20 seconds until melted.

3. Dump the next 5 ingredients into the bowl and stir to combine.

4. Place the remaining ingredients in a large roasting pan and stir to combine.

5. Pour the melted butter mixture over the dry ingredients in the roasting pan and stir to coat.

6. Bake for about 45 minutes, stirring every 10 to 15 minutes, until crispy and browned.

THE FARMER IN THE DILL

You know you're a mom when the nursery rhymes have officially infiltrated what few brain cells you feel like you have left. You knew it was bound to happen, but you didn't think it would happen while reading a cocktail book. At this point, you're just going to have to embrace it. I don't think it's going to go away anytime soon. Just plop your kid into their high chair and sing together (as you make this cocktail).

MAKES 1 SERVING

Ingredients

5–7 slices cucumber, thinly sliced
6 dill sprigs, plus extra to garnish
½ ounce lime juice
½ ounce simple syrup
2 ounces tequila
Ice
4 ounces ginger beer
Lime wedge, to garnish

Instructions

1. Combine the sliced cucumber and the dill in a cocktail shaker and muddle.

2. Add the lime juice, simple syrup, tequila, and ice.

3. Shake until chilled.

4. Strain into an ice-filled tall glass and top with ginger beer.

5. Garnish with the lime wedge and another sprig of dill.

THE HORSERADISH ONE

Yes, horseradish. Hear me out. It's just a little bit, and I promise it doesn't overpower the other flavors in the recipe. The spicy horseradish pairs perfectly with the herbal gin and is mellowed by the cool cucumber, and the simple syrup and lime juice help to sweeten and brighten this cocktail up.

MAKES 1 SERVING

Ingredients

4 slices cucumber

Pinch salt

½ ounce simple syrup

1½ teaspoons prepared horseradish

3 ounces gin

1 ounce lime juice

Ice

Cucumber wheel, to garnish

Instructions

1. In a cocktail shaker, muddle the cucumber, salt, simple syrup, and horseradish.

2. Add the gin, lime juice, and ice.

3. Shake until well combined and chilled.

4. Double strain into a coupe glass.

5. Garnish with a cucumber wheel.

CHAPTER 3
Sweet & Sugary

DRUNK MONKEY

This drink mentally transports me to an all-inclusive resort on a tropical island with a warm breeze and sea salt in the air . . . or maybe just a hibachi restaurant where you get to take home the fun ceramic drinking glass. It's the perfect indulgence for a summer day (and if you put it in the same cup your toddler is drinking out of, you can tell them that you're drinking chocolate milk, too).

MAKES 1 SERVING

Ingredients

Chocolate syrup, to garnish (*not* optional!)

1 ounce chocolate vodka

1 teaspoon espresso vodka

1 ounce banana liqueur

1 teaspoon coffee liqueur

1 ounce cream or milk

Ice

Instructions

1. Drizzle a chilled glass of your choice with chocolate syrup and set aside.

2. Combine the vodka, banana liqueur, coffee liqueur, and cream in an ice-filled cocktail shaker.

3. Shake until chilled.

4. Strain into glass.

ESPRESSO MARTINI

If it looks like coffee and tastes like coffee, it must be coffee . . . right? At least that's what you can say when you roll into the meeting ten minutes late with one of these in your #1 Mom travel mug.

MAKES 1 SERVING

Ingredients

1 ounce chilled espresso or cold brew concentrate

1 ounce vanilla vodka

½ ounce Irish cream

½ ounce coffee liqueur

Splash hazelnut liqueur

Ice

Instructions

1. Combine the espresso, vodka, Irish cream, coffee liqueur, and hazelnut liqueur in an ice-filled cocktail shaker.

2. Shake until chilled.

3. Strain into a chilled coupe or martini glass.

RICE KRISPIES TREATS™ SHAKE

With Rice Krispies Treats™ being basically the only dessert my mom knew how to make when I was growing up, they will forever remind me of my childhood. If you're like me and inherited your mom's baking abilities (or lack thereof), go ahead and use the premade version in this cocktail.

MAKES 2 SERVINGS

Ingredients

6 ounces milk

4 ounces vanilla vodka

2 cups vanilla ice cream

⅓ cup marshmallow fluff

2 Rice Krispies Treats™ (broken into small pieces)

Instructions

1. Combine the milk, vodka, ice cream, marshmallow fluff, and Rice Krispies Treats™ in a blender.

2. Blend until smooth.

3. Divide into two large glasses and serve with a spoon and/or straw.

SALTED CARAMEL MARTINI

Things I can't say no to: puppies, Cheetos, another glass of wine, and salted caramel. And fun fact: there is a scientifically proven reason as to why we (because I know I'm not the only one) just can't get enough of salty caramelly goodness. It's called hedonic escalation, which is apparently a fancy term for feel-good stuff happening in your brain when you eat something as delectable as this perfect combination of sweet, salty, and fatty. Just imagine the goodness that will happen in that brain of yours when you throw some booze in the mix!

MAKES 1 SERVING

Ingredients

Caramel syrup and salt, to rim the glass

Ice

1½ ounces vanilla vodka

1 ounce butternut schnapps

2 ounces RumChata

Instructions

1. Pour a small pool of caramel syrup and salt on a plate or shallow bowl and roll the rim of a coupe or martini glass in the salted caramel.

2. Drizzle additional caramel into the glass, if desired.

3. In an ice-filled cocktail shaker, combine the vodka, schnapps, and RumChata.

4. Shake until chilled and strain into the prepared glass.

CHRISTMAS IN MEXICO

Imagine it's Christmas Day and you're sitting on the beach with a drink in your hand and not sitting on the couch assembling all those toys your kid will only play with twice. I'll drink to that.

MAKES 2 SERVINGS

Ingredients

Chocolate syrup, to garnish

Ice

6 ounces light coconut milk

2 ounces tequila

2 ounces coffee liqueur

1 teaspoon simple syrup

Dash cinnamon

Dash cayenne pepper

Instructions

1. Drizzle chocolate syrup on the inside of two rocks glasses.

2. Fill glasses with ice and set aside.

3. In an ice-filled cocktail shaker, combine the coconut milk, tequila, coffee liqueur, simple syrup, cinnamon, and cayenne pepper.

4. Shake until chilled and strain into prepared glasses.

JUST PEACHY

An Instagram-worthy cocktail so pretty and delicious I put it on the cover of this book.

MAKES 1 SERVING

Ingredients

1½ ounces light rum

½ ounce peach schnapps

½ ounce coconut rum

2 dashes orange bitters

Ice

Instructions

1. Combine the light rum, schnapps, coconut rum, and bitters in an ice-filled cocktail shaker.

2. Shake until chilled.

3. Strain into a chilled martini glass.

COFFEE & COLA

If you like vanilla iced coffee and cola floats, you'll love this perfect boozy love child of the two! Serve as described below or swap out the cream or milk for a scoop of vanilla ice cream. Either way, you can't go wrong, and it will make sitting in the ninety-degrees-at-nine-in-the-morning summer heat while your kid plays outside infinitely more bearable.

MAKES 1 SERVING

Ingredients

Ice
1 ounce vanilla vodka
1 ounce coffee liqueur
7½ ounces cola
Splash cream or milk

Instructions

1. Fill a pint glass with ice and pour in the vodka and coffee liqueur.

2. Add the cola and top with a floater of cream or milk.

3. Gently stir and serve with a straw.

WHITE CHOCOLATE COLADA

I'm a big fan of the non-chocolate Piña Colada (especially poolside) but the white chocolate in this version takes it to another level of indulgence.

MAKES 1 SERVING

Ingredients

1 ounce white rum
1 ounce white chocolate liqueur
1 ounce coconut cream
3½ ounces pineapple juice
Ice

Instructions

1. Combine all ingredients in a blender.

2. Blend until smooth.

PB&R

This is a weird one. But you probably already have all the ingredients, so why not give it a shot? Put the kid to bed early and try this one out. You might be pleasantly surprised. And if not, dump it down the drain, flip the page, and try another one.

MAKES 1 SERVING

Ingredients

1 spoonful smooth peanut butter

2 ounces vodka

¼ ounce cinnamon schnapps

½ ounce coconut rum

1½ ounces apple juice

1½ ounces pineapple juice

¾ ounce lime juice

Ice

Instructions

1. Drop peanut butter into the bottom of a cocktail shaker.

2. Add the rest of the ingredients.

3. Shake and strain into an ice-filled tall glass.

PRO MOM TIP

Give peanut butter powder a try instead of traditional peanut butter for a smoother cocktail, or peanut butter-flavored vodka instead of the peanut butter and vodka for an even easier recipe.

SPARKLING BERRY FLOAT

Okay, so, there's not actually any ice cream in this. But I won't judge you if you add some! The white chocolate liqueur combined with the jam and grenadine only makes it seem like you're indulging in a luxurious ice cream float. It's the perfect dessert cocktail for when you're looking for something fruity, silky, and just a little chocolaty.

MAKES 1 SERVING

Ingredients

Ice

4 ounces rosé wine

1 ounce white chocolate liqueur

1 tablespoon raspberry or strawberry jam

1 teaspoon grenadine

Strawberry slice, to garnish

Instructions

1. Fill a glass of your choice with ice and set aside.

2. Combine the rosé, white chocolate liqueur, jam, and grenadine in an ice-filled cocktail shaker.

3. Shake until chilled.

4. Pour into the prepared glass.

5. Garnish with a strawberry slice.

COOKIES & CREAMTINI

There are few flavor combinations in life better than cookies and cream, except when you mix them with the rest of the ingredients below into a frosty, boozy, milkshakey concoction. For the sake of keeping grubby little fingers out of your cocktail, make your kid a nonalcoholic version first so you can enjoy yours in peace.

MAKES 4 COCKTAILS (OR 2 *REALLY* BIG ONES)

Ingredients

12 chocolate sandwich cookies

4 ounces hazelnut liqueur

4 ounces coffee liqueur

4 ounces Irish cream

4 ounces heavy whipping cream

1 tablespoon honey

Ice

Instructions

1. Place the sandwich cookies into a resealable plastic bag.

2. Seal the bag and crush cookies until finely crushed.

3. Place all the ingredients, including the crushed cookies, in a blender.

4. Blend well.

5. Serve in a chilled fountain glass.

ADULT APPLE JUICE

Step 1: Don't mix up your cup with your kid's cup.

MAKES 1 SERVING

Ingredients

1½ ounces vanilla vodka
½ ounce whisky
½ ounce apple schnapps
½ ounce dry vermouth
½ ounce apple juice
Dash cinnamon
1 teaspoon simple syrup
Ice

Instructions

1. Combine the vodka, whisky, schnapps, vermouth, apple juice, cinnamon, and simple syrup in an ice-filled cocktail shaker.

2. Shake until chilled and strain into a chilled coupe glass.

CHOCOLATE & ORANGE

Do you remember those chocolate oranges you'd buy from the grocery store that you slam onto the table to separate the "slices"? I loved those things. I have no idea if they are still made anymore or why they remind me of the holidays, but this is the cocktail version of those!

MAKES 1 SERVING

Ingredients

2 ounces vodka

½ ounce triple sec

1 tablespoon orange zest

1 teaspoon hot cocoa powder

1 dash orange bitters

Ice

Instructions

1. Combine the vodka, triple sec, orange zest, hot cocoa powder, and bitters in an ice-filled cocktail shaker.

2. Shake until chilled and strain into a chilled coupe glass.

SUGAR COOKIE MARTINI

There are two types of people in this world: the type who like the frosted sugar cookies from the grocery store that are festively frosted for each holiday, and the type who don't. While these types may be divided, I'm hoping we can all agree on a martini that tastes just like a sugar cookie.

MAKES 1 SERVING

Ingredients

Sprinkles, to garnish
1 ounce amaretto
1½ ounces RumChata
Ice
1½ ounces vanilla vodka

Instructions

1. Pour a small pool of sprinkles onto a plate or bowl.

2. Use the amaretto or RumChata to wet the rim of a martini glass and roll the rim of the glass in the sprinkles. Set aside.

3. In an ice-filled cocktail shaker, combine the vodka, amaretto, and RumChata.

4. Shake until chilled and strain into a prepared martini glass.

PRETTY IN PINK

Try to tell me this isn't the cutest cocktail you've ever seen! Perfect for a girls' night in.

MAKES 1 SERVING

Ingredients

Strawberry syrup

1 scoop vanilla ice cream

1½ ounces gin

1 teaspoon grenadine

1 ounce milk

Instructions

1. Drizzle the inside of a martini glass with strawberry syrup.

2. Place the ice cream in the bottom of the glass.

3. Combine the gin, grenadine, and milk in a cocktail shaker.

4. Shake to combine and pour over the ice cream.

CHAPTER 4

Sharing Is Caring (But I Won't Judge If You Don't!)

CHAMPAGNE SLUSHIE

This recipe takes me back to my college days when I felt rich with $100 in my bank account, didn't have any bills or responsibilities, and definitely didn't have a mini-me running around. A variation of a popular drink made at one of my college hangouts, this Champagne Slushie is a perfect patio sipper that you'll want to share with your girlfriends over brunch.

MAKES 4 SERVINGS

Ingredients

2 cups frozen peach slices
2 cups ice
2 ounces peach schnapps
1 ounce pomegranate or cherry-flavored cocktail syrup
6 ounces sparkling wine

Instructions

1. Combine the peaches, ice, peach schnapps, and syrup in a blender and blend on high for 30 seconds or until smooth.

2. Add the sparkling wine and pulse until combined.

PRO MOM TIP

Make your kid one of those healthy butternut squash, peach, banana, whatever smoothies, then make yourself one of these and pour into identical glasses. They'll never know!

SHARING IS CARING

MORGARITA

A margarita recipe I received from a good friend that I renamed *Morgarita*, because you'll be left wanting more. Classy, authentic, and complex . . . three words you will not use to describe this recipe. However, if you're just looking for a damn good margarita recipe, this is the one! Kinda frozen, kinda not, and just the right balance of sweet and tart.

MAKES ABOUT 8 SERVINGS

Ingredients

1 can frozen limeade concentrate

1 empty limeade can ice

1 empty limeade can tequila

½ empty limeade can of orange-flavored liqueur

24 ounces lager beer

Instructions

1. Place the frozen limeade concentrate in a blender and use that empty can as the measuring device for the ice, tequila, and orange liqueur. Add the ice, tequila, and orange liqueur to the blender.

2. Make sure no one is looking and add more tequila.

3. Blend for 30 seconds on high or until smooth.

4. Add the beer to the blender and pulse until combined.

PRO MOM TIP

Add a cocktail umbrella so you can pretend you're floating in a resort pool in Mexico instead of hiding from your toddler in the kitchen.

LEMON BERRY COOLER

My husband and I generally enjoy the same types of foods, but when it comes to cocktails and our wedding cake flavor (which happened to be lemon berry), our preferences are pretty opposite. Glad I won't have to share this one.

MAKES ABOUT 15–20 SERVINGS

Ingredients

1⅔ cups lemon juice

1⅔ cups simple syrup

2 cups strawberries, halved and destemmed

1 (750-ml.) bottle vodka

Ice

1 (750 ml.) bottle sparkling wine

Strawberry slices, to garnish

Instructions

1. In a blender, combine the lemon juice, simple syrup, strawberries, and vodka.

2. Blend until smooth.

3. Serve over ice and top with the sparkling wine.

4. Garnish with strawberry slices.

FISH HOUSE PUNCH

1770s: The Revolutionary War, the adoption of the Declaration of Independence, and the creation of the Fish House Punch. Yes, this cocktail is really that old. It has been said that this drink was created to celebrate women being allowed into the Fish House, a gentlemen's social club, for the first time. Enjoy this batch cocktail with your best girlfriends—no men allowed.

MAKES ABOUT 10 SERVINGS

Ingredients

3 cups dark rum

1½ cups brandy

1½ cups simple syrup

1½ cups lemon juice

¾ cup peach schnapps

3 cups cold water

Ice

Instructions

1. Combine the rum, brandy, simple syrup, lemon juice, schnapps, and water in a pitcher, punch bowl, or beverage dispenser.

2. Serve over ice.

IT WAS ALL A DREAMSICLE

If you didn't just sing to yourself "I used to read *Word Up!* magazine" then you definitely can't sit with me. Turn on the old-school hip-hop radio station and drink up, b*tches.

MAKES ABOUT 10 SERVINGS

Ingredients

1 cup vanilla vodka

½ cup triple sec

4 cups orange juice

4 cups vanilla ice cream

Ice

Instructions

1. Combine all ingredients in a blender.

2. Blend until smooth and serve immediately.

ROSÉ PUNCH

Rosé punch, the ever-so-slightly more sophisticated older sister of the Morgarita (page 100). The same concept is used for both: frozen fruit juice concentrate and an effervescent, but the pink color and sparkling wine kicks the fanciness level up a couple notches.

MAKES ABOUT 10 SERVINGS

Ingredients

1 bottle rosé wine (still or sparkling)
1 cup blueberries (fresh or frozen)
1 (12-ounce) can frozen pink lemonade,
slightly thawed
1 liter club soda or lemon-lime soda

Instructions

1. In a large pitcher, combine the wine, blueberries, and frozen pink lemonade.

2. If time (and patience) allows, set in refrigerator for 1 hour.

3. Pour into champagne flutes and top with the soda.

COOL AS A CUCUMBER

As I write this recipe, there lie several orphan cucumbers in the break room at work. Coincidence? I think not.

MAKES ABOUT 15–20 SERVINGS

Ingredients

2 cups cucumbers, peeled and diced

Small handful mint leaves

6 cups vodka

4 cups lime juice

3 cups simple syrup

1 cup cold water

Ice

Basil and mint, to garnish

Instructions

1. Combine the cucumbers, mint, vodka, lime juice, simple syrup, and water in a blender and blend until smooth.

2. Strain into a large pitcher or bowl.

3. Serve over ice.

4. Garnish with basil and mint leaves.

SHARING IS CARING

JAMAICAN ME CRAZY

If it's not your kid, significant other, dog, or family that is Jamaican you crazy then this drink will. But in a good way. A way that will leave you wanting more of this sweet summer cocktail (and a pool to enjoy it in).

MAKES ABOUT 8 SERVINGS

Ingredients

2 cups coconut rum
½ cup orange-flavored liqueur
1 cup pineapple juice
½ cup lime juice
½ cup simple syrup
Ice
Fresh jalapeño, sliced (optional)

Instructions

1. Combine the rum, orange liqueur, fruit juices, and simple syrup in a small serving pitcher and stir.

2. Fill rocks glasses with ice and garnish with a fresh jalapeño.

3. Pour the cocktail mixture into prepared glasses and enjoy!

PUMPKIN PIE

Go ahead and call me stereotypical and whisper "of course you do" after what I'm about to say, but I love pumpkin spice. And what could possibly be better than combining pumpkin spice with a little bit of vodka? Nothing. Well, other than being able to enjoy it in peace.

MAKES ABOUT 10 SERVINGS

Ingredients

½ gallon apple cider
1 (15-ounce) can pumpkin puree
1 (12-ounce) can cream soda
1 teaspoon pumpkin pie spice
1 cup vanilla vodka
Ice
Vanilla ice cream (optional)

Instructions

1. Combine the apple cider, pumpkin puree, cream soda, pumpkin pie spice, and vodka in a blender.

2. Blend until smooth and serve over ice.

3. Serve over ice cream (if using), float style!

GRAPE EXPECTATIONS

I'm not generally a fan of grape-flavored things (unless it's wine but does that even count?) but the lime and rum in this cocktail are the true stars of this show. Garnish this cocktail with a skewer of grapes and give yourself a pat on the back for having your fruit for the day!

MAKES ABOUT 6 SERVINGS

Ingredients

2 limes, quartered

20 seedless red grapes, halved, plus extra to garnish

3 ounces simple syrup

1 cup light rum

1 cup club soda

Ice

Instructions

1. Place the lime pieces and grapes in a cocktail shaker and muddle.

2. Add the simple syrup, rum, club soda, and ice to the cocktail shaker.

3. Shake until chilled, then double strain into prepared rocks glasses.

4. Garnish with a skewer of grapes.

PRO MOM TIP

Add a couple mint leaves into the shaker with the fruit and muddle together for a twist on a classic Mojito.

PINEAPPLE RUM MULE

A grown-up version of something you and your college roommates would have thrown together for a tiki-themed party.

MAKES ABOUT 8 SERVINGS

Ingredients

1 cup lime juice

2 cups ginger beer

3 cups dark rum

2 cups pineapple juice

Ice

Instructions

1. Combine the lime juice, ginger beer, rum, and pineapple juice in a pitcher and stir to combine.

2. Serve over ice.

SELTZERITA

A lighter and fizzier version of my Morgarita (page 100), these are perfect for sipping poolside all day with your girlfriends.

MAKES ABOUT 6 SERVINGS

Ingredients

6 ounces lime juice, *divided*

Coarse salt, to rim the glass

Ice

1½ cups silver tequila

2 ounces simple syrup

4 ounces orange juice

Splash lime-flavored seltzer water

Instructions

1. Wet the rim of a rocks or margarita glass with lime juice.

2. Pour a small pool of salt onto a plate or shallow dish and roll the rim of each glass into the salt to coat.

3. Fill glasses with ice and set aside.

4. Combine the tequila, remaining lime juice, simple syrup, and orange juice into a pitcher and stir to combine.

5. Pour mixture into prepared glasses and top with the seltzer water to taste.

ARNOLD'S COUSIN

This can easily be made into a fun, frosty, alcohol-free version (for the kids, not you!) if you feel so inclined. Otherwise, Arnold's Cousin is another one of those perfect patio/pool sippers.

MAKES ABOUT 10–15 SERVINGS

Ingredients

7 cups water

½ cup simple syrup

1 (12-ounce) can frozen orange juice concentrate

1 (12-ounce) can frozen lemonade concentrate

2 cups cold black tea

2 cups bourbon

Splash lemon-lime soda

Instructions

1. Combine the water, simple syrup, orange and lemonade concentrates, cold black tea, and bourbon in a blender.

2. Blend until smooth.

3. Serve in a tall glass and top with lemon-lime soda to taste.

MULLED MERLOT

This will make your house smell so good. So Autumny. So sweater weather. So crunchy leaves on the ground that you desperately offer the neighbor kid $20 to rake up.

MAKES ABOUT 10–15 SERVINGS

Ingredients

2 (750-ml.) bottles merlot
½ cup sugar
1 cup orange juice
½ cup brandy
4 cinnamon sticks
1 orange, halved
4 whole cloves

Instructions

1. Combine the merlot, sugar, orange juice, brandy, and cinnamon sticks in a large slow cooker.

2. Spike ½ orange with the cloves and add it to the slow cooker.

3. Cut the other half of the orange into pieces or slices and add them to the slow cooker.

4. Stir everything until combined.

5. Cook on low for an hour.

6. Serve warm.

PARTY THYME

Inspired by an orange and thyme scented candle I had, I present to you the Party Thyme. I'd much rather have a pitcher of this on my counter than a candle that my kid will inevitably knock off the table and break.

MAKES ABOUT 10–15 SERVINGS

Ingredients

4 sprigs thyme

6 ounces simple syrup

1 (750 ml) bottle dry white wine

1½ cups citrus vodka

3 cups no-pulp orange juice

3 ounces lemon juice

1 teaspoon vanilla extract

Ice

Splash club soda

Instructions

1. Combine the thyme and simple syrup in a cocktail shaker.

2. Muddle and strain into a pitcher, discarding the sprigs and any leaves that may have slipped through.

3. Add the wine, vodka, orange juice, lemon juice, and vanilla extract to the pitcher and stir to combine.

4. Pour into ice-filled glasses and top with club soda as desired.

ACKNOWLEDGMENTS

A huge thank-you goes out to everyone that contributed to the completion of this book whether it was by encouraging me, helping me, or drinking with me along the way. I couldn't have done it without you!

To Rick Luettke: With an eye for perfection and a love of bourbon, you made sure each cocktail was captured beautifully. Thank you!

To John Jacob: The person who knows more about booze than I ever thought there was to know. Thank you for making sure each cocktail was poured and garnished to perfection.

To my husband, parents, and Kelly and Bill: Thank you for being my taste testers and biggest cheerleaders along the way.

CONVERSION CHART

Metric and Imperial Conversions

(These conversions are rounded for convenience)

Ingredient	Cups/ Tablespoons/ Teaspoons	Ounces	Grams/ Milliliters
Fruit, dried	1 cup	4 ounces	120 grams
Fruits or veggies, chopped	1 cup	5 to 7 ounces	145 to 200 grams
Fruits or veggies, pureed	1 cup	8.5 ounces	245 grams
Honey, maple syrup, or corn syrup	1 tablespoon	0.75 ounce	20 grams
Liquids: cream, milk, water, or juice	1 cup	8 fluid ounces	240 milliliters
Salt	1 teaspoon	0.2 ounces	6 grams
Spices: cinnamon, cloves, ginger, or nutmeg (ground)	1 teaspoon	0.2 ounce	5 milliliters
Sugar, brown, firmly packed	1 cup	7 ounces	200 grams
Sugar, white	1 cup/1 tablespoon	7 ounces/0.5 ounce	200 grams/12.5 grams
Vanilla extract	1 teaspoon	0.2 ounce	4 grams

Liquids

8 fluid ounces = 1 cup = ½ pint
16 fluid ounces = 2 cups = 1 pint
32 fluid ounces = 4 cups = 1 quart
128 fluid ounces = 16 cups = 1 gallon

INDEX